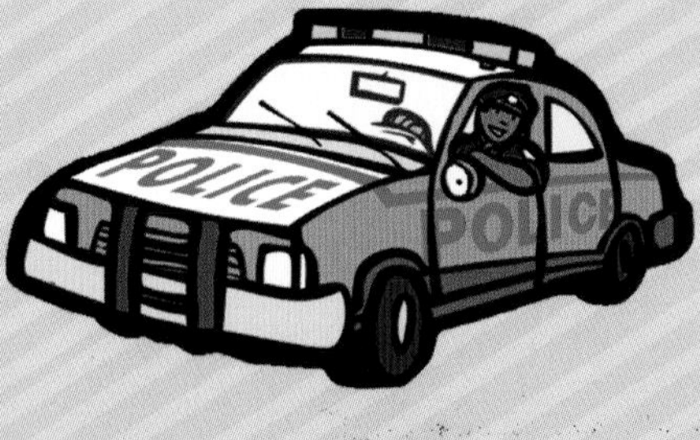
POLICE
POLICE

FIRST GRAPHICS

MY COMMUNITY

A VISIT TO THE POLICE STATION

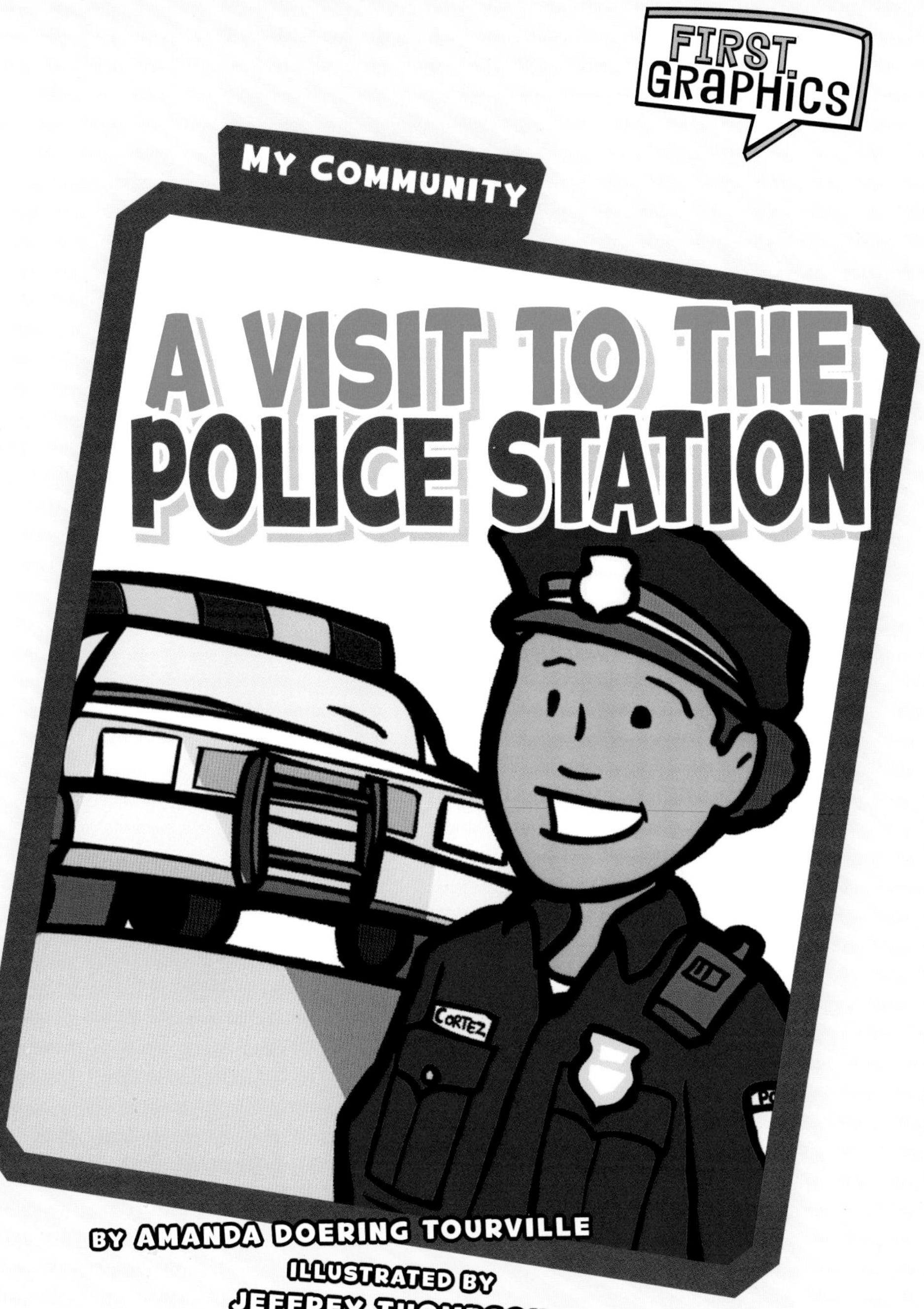
CORTEZ

BY AMANDA DOERING TOURVILLE

ILLUSTRATED BY

JEFFREY THOMPSON

Consultant: Mark G. Robbins, PhD
Department of Government
Minnesota State University, Mankato

CAPSTONE PRESS
a capstone imprint

First Graphics are published by Capstone Press,
151 Good Counsel Drive, P.O. Box 669, Mankato, Minnesota 56002.
www.capstonepub.com

Books published by Capstone Press are manufactured with paper
containing at least 10 percent post-consumer waste.

Library of Congress Cataloging-in-Publication Data
Tourville, Amanda Doering, 1980-
A visit to the police station / by Amanda Doering Tourville ; illustrated by Jeffrey
Thompson.
    p. cm. — (First graphics. My community)
ISBN 978-1-4296-5369-5 (library binding)
ISBN 978-1-4296-6235-2 (paperback)
1. Police—Juvenile literature. 2. Police stations—Juvenile literature. 3. Graphic
novels. I. Thompson, Jeffrey (Jeffrey Allen), 1970- II. Title. III. Series.

HV7922.T68 2011
363.2—dc22
                                                    2010026697

Editor: **Shelly Lyons**
Designer: **Alison Thiele**
Art Director: **Nathan Gassman**
Production Specialist: **Eric Manske**

Printed in the United States of America in
Stevens Point, Wisconsin.
092010   005934WZS11

TABLE OF CONTENTS

Irvin L. Young Memorial Library
Whitewater, Wisconsin

To Protect and Serve

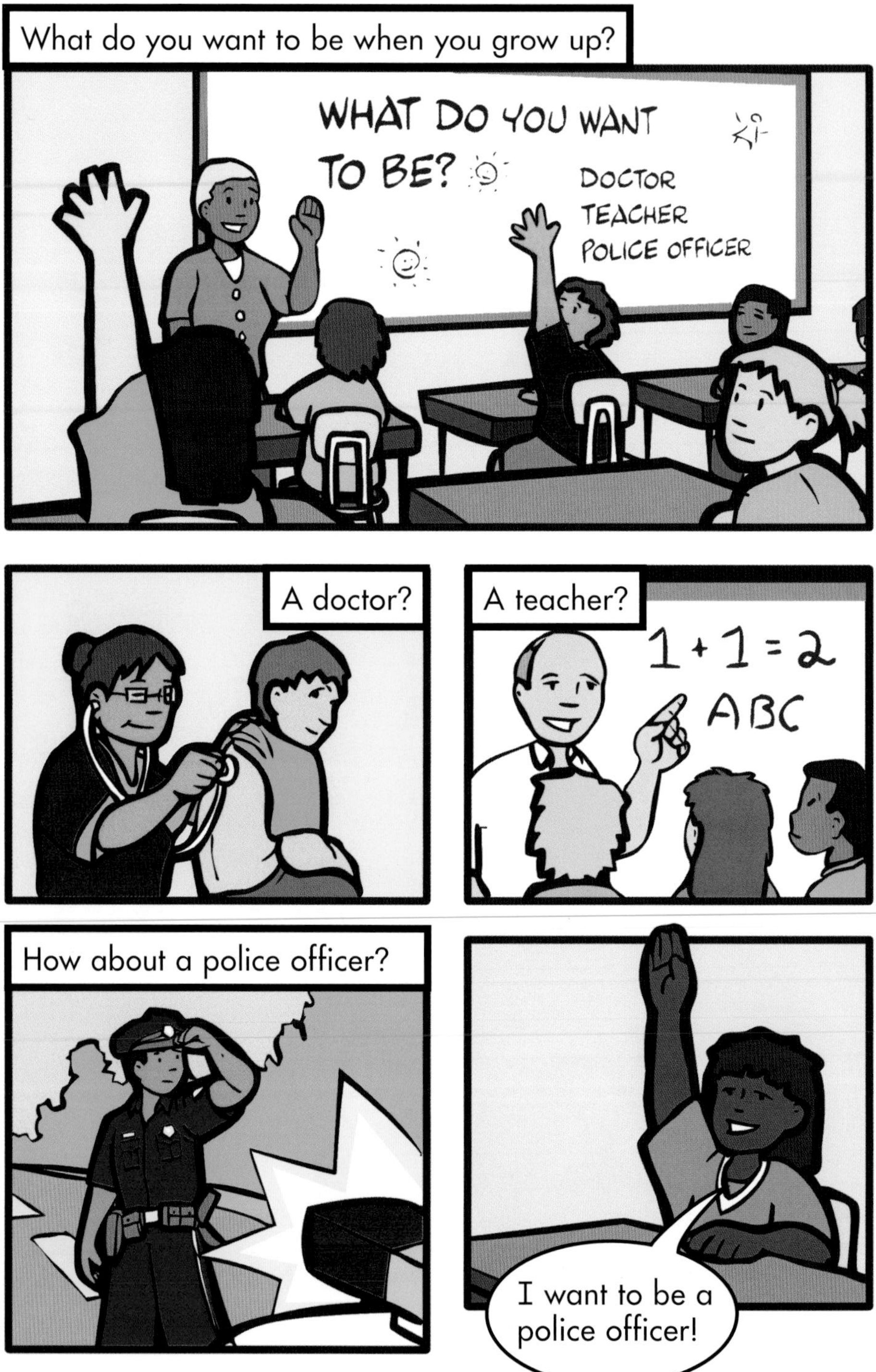
What do you want to be when you grow up?
WHAT DO YOU WANT TO BE?
DOCTOR
TEACHER
POLICE OFFICER
A doctor?
A teacher?
1 + 1 = 2
ABC
How about a police officer?
I want to be a police officer!

Police officers keep our communities safe.
They make sure people follow laws.

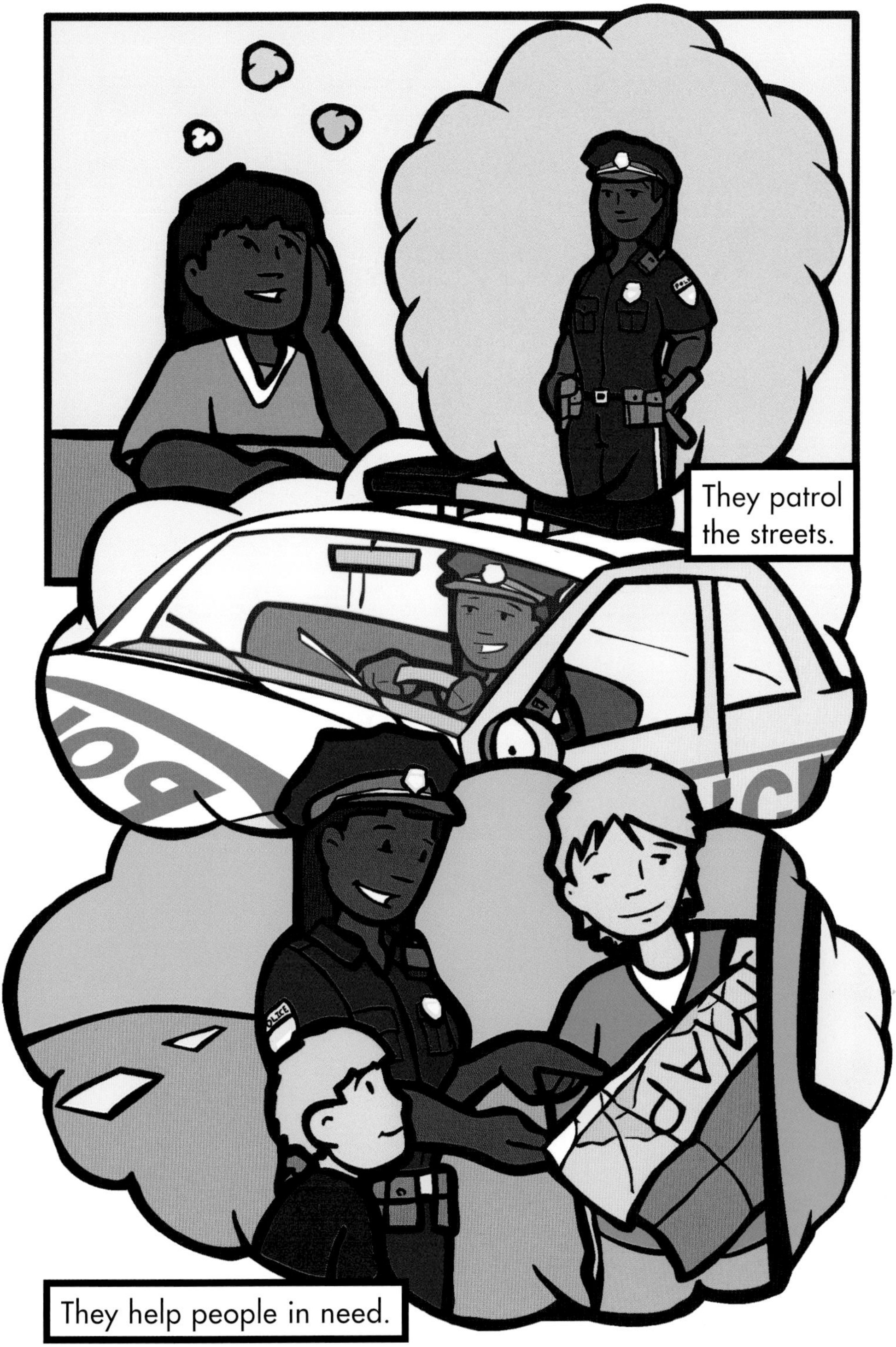
They patrol the streets.
They help people in need.

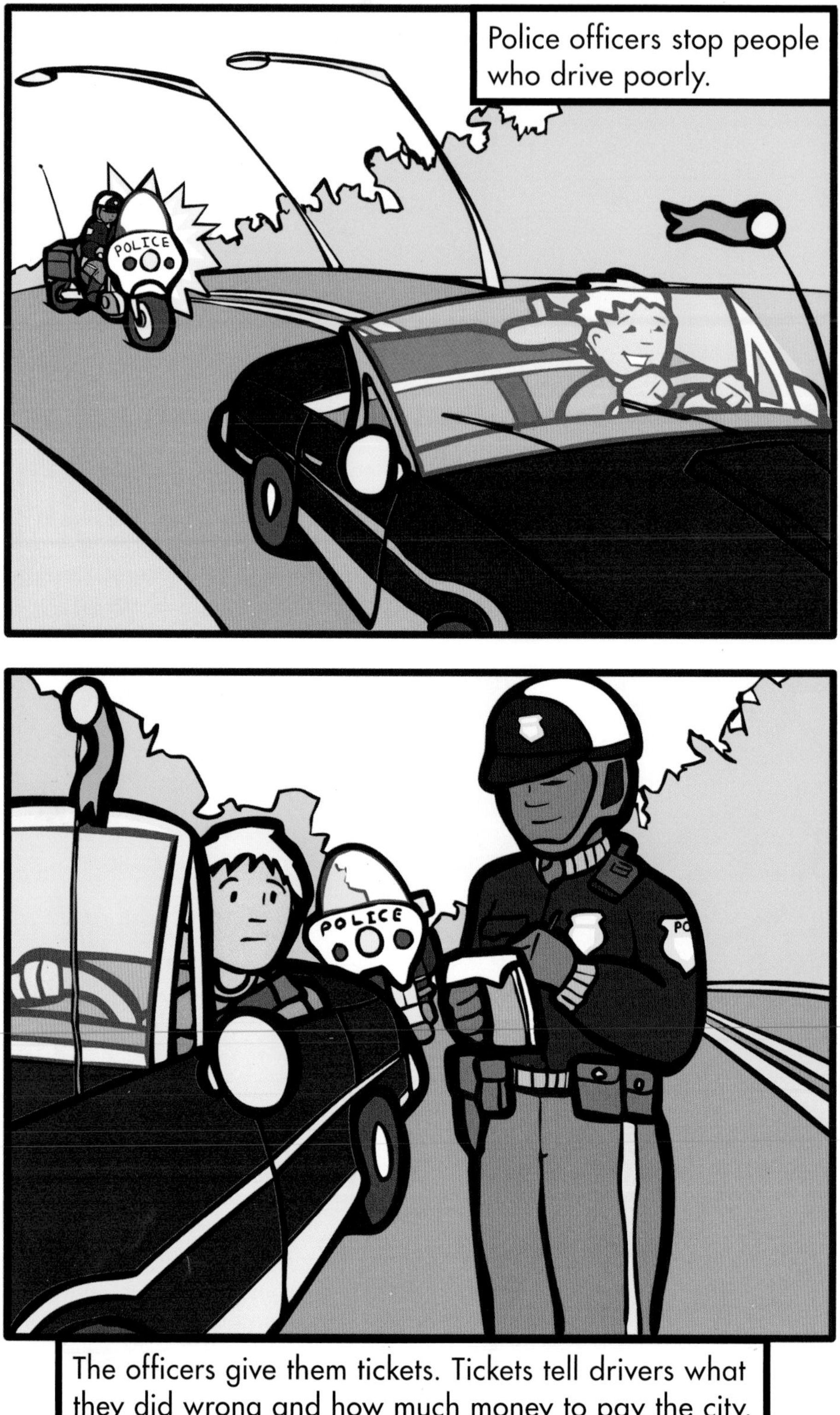
Police officers stop people who drive poorly.
POLICE
POLICE
The officers give them tickets. Tickets tell drivers what they did wrong and how much money to pay the city.

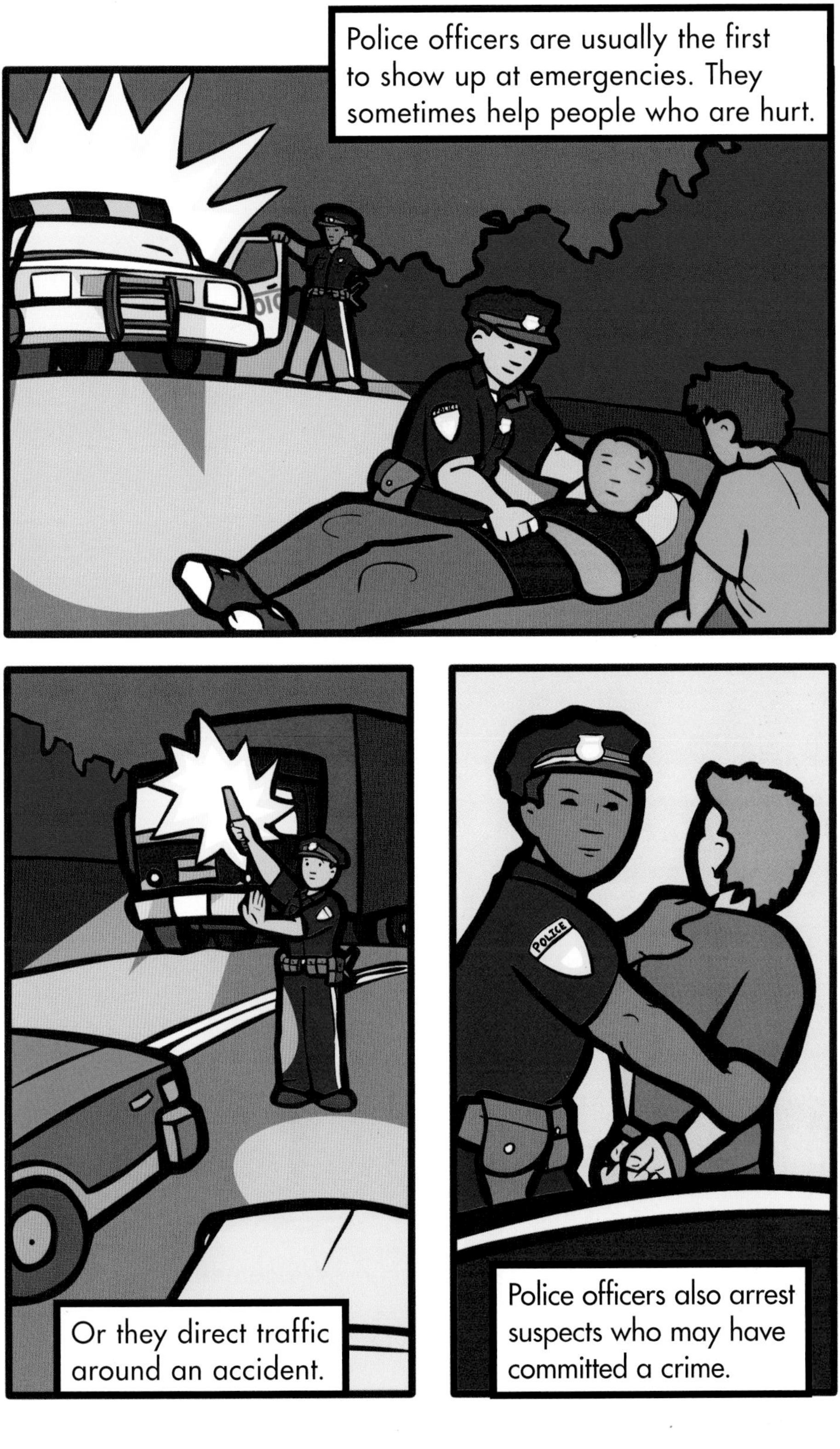
Police officers are usually the first to show up at emergencies. They sometimes help people who are hurt.
Or they direct traffic around an accident.
POLICE
Police officers also arrest suspects who may have committed a crime.

ARRIVING AT THE STATION

Nicole's class is visiting the police station.

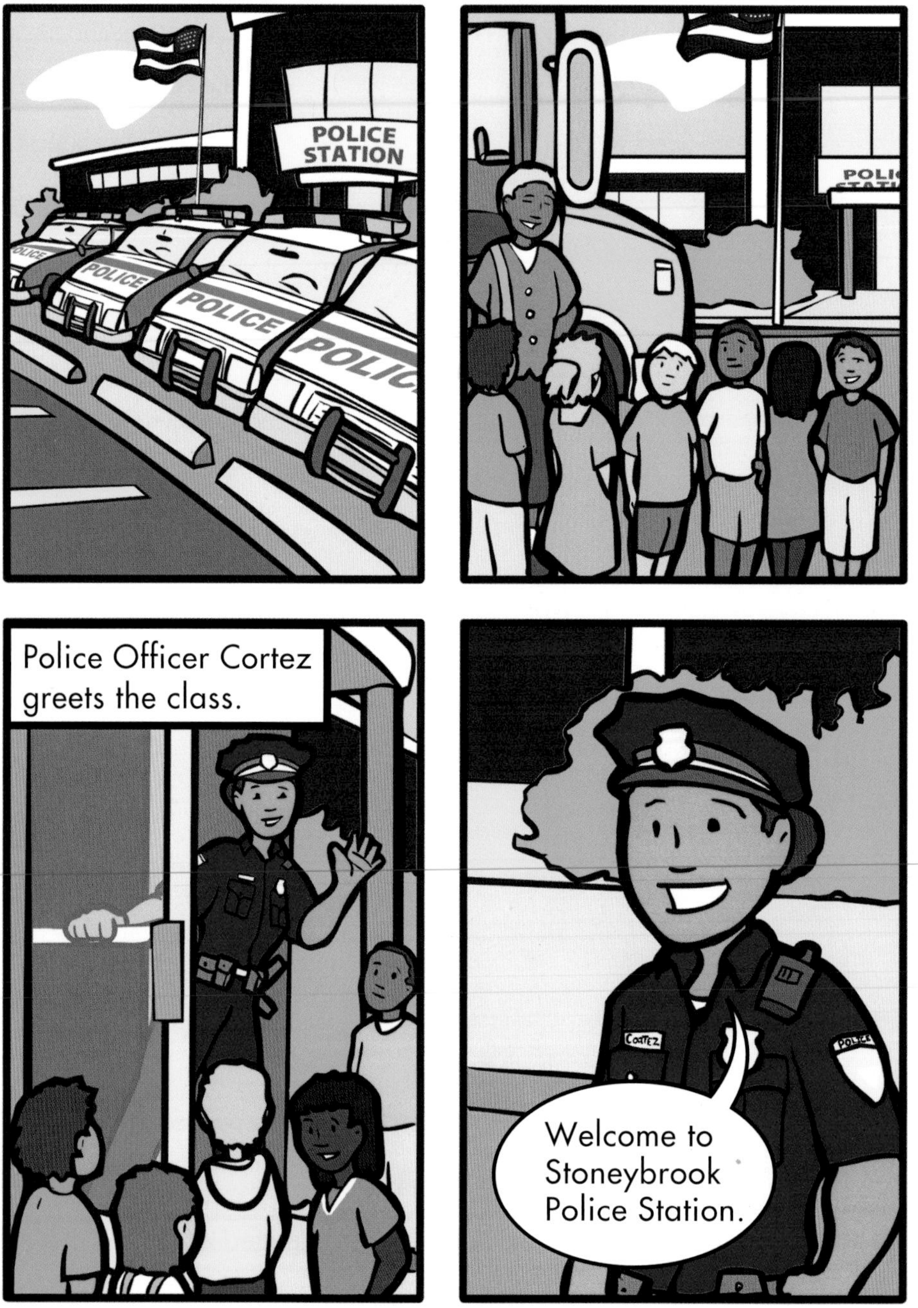
POLICE STATION
POLICE
Police Officer Cortez greets the class.
CORTEZ
Welcome to Stoneybrook Police Station.

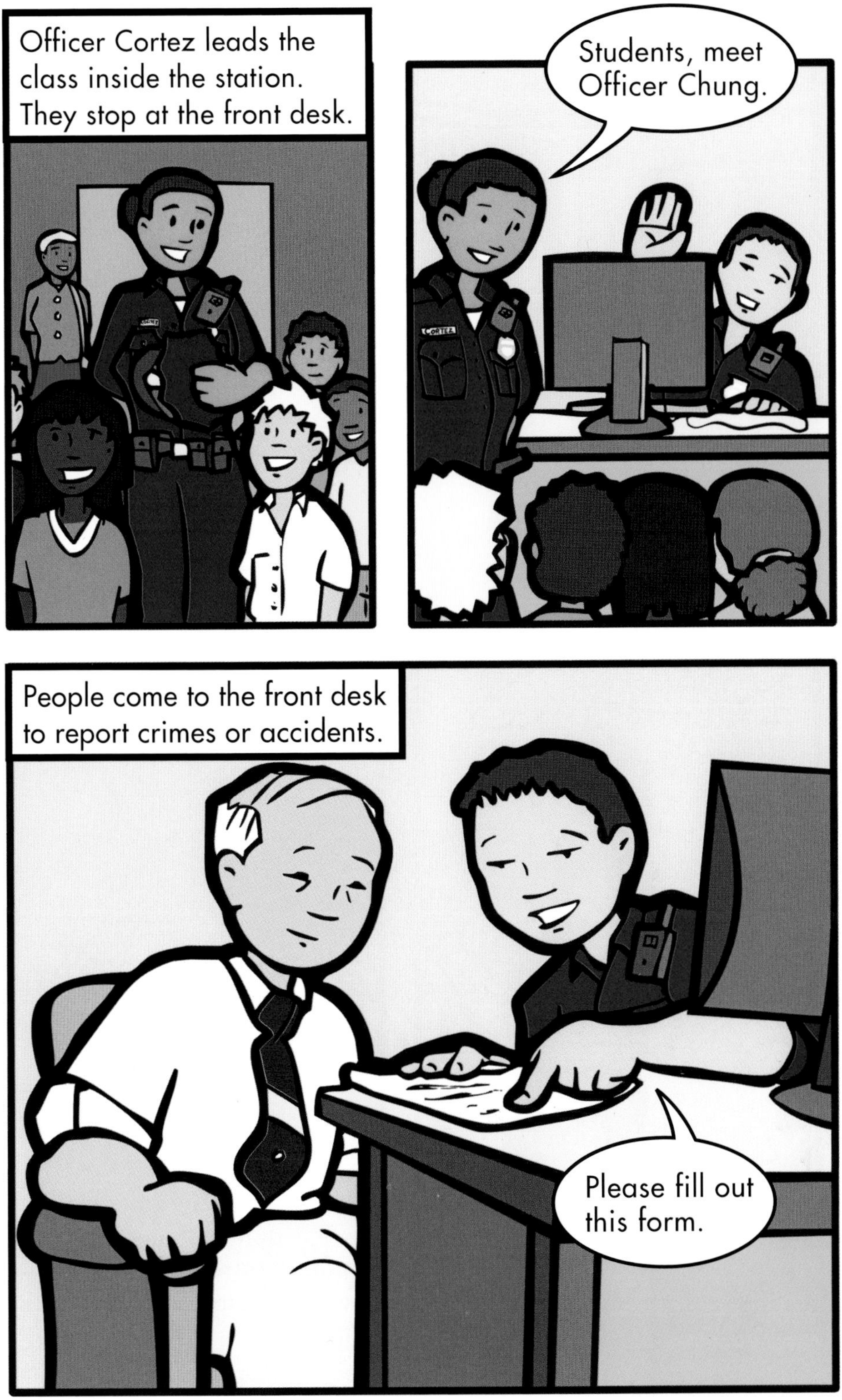
Officer Cortez leads the class inside the station. They stop at the front desk.
Students, meet Officer Chung.
CORTEZ
People come to the front desk to report crimes or accidents.
Please fill out this form.

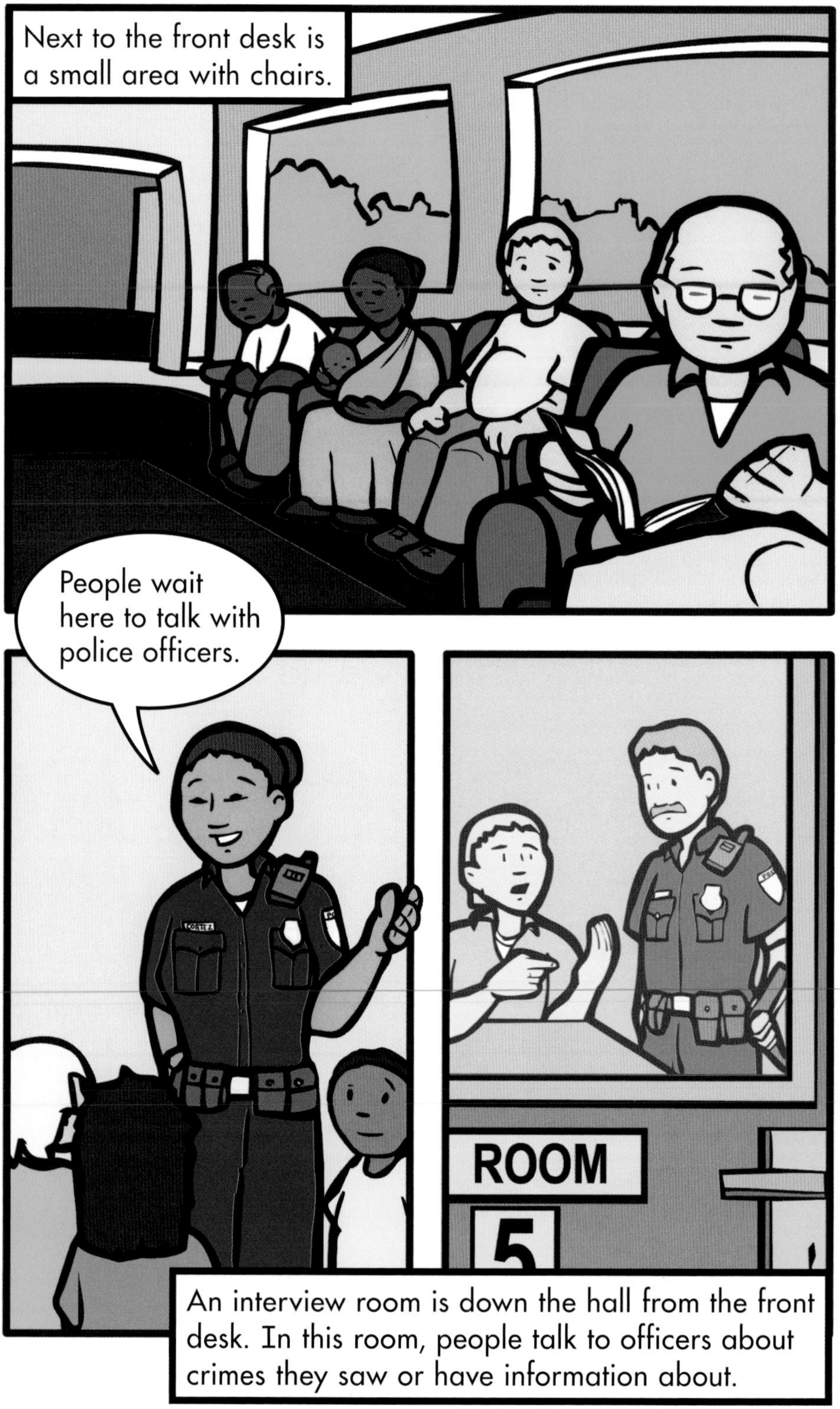
Next to the front desk is a small area with chairs.
People wait here to talk with police officers.
ROOM
5
An interview room is down the hall from the front desk. In this room, people talk to officers about crimes they saw or have information about.

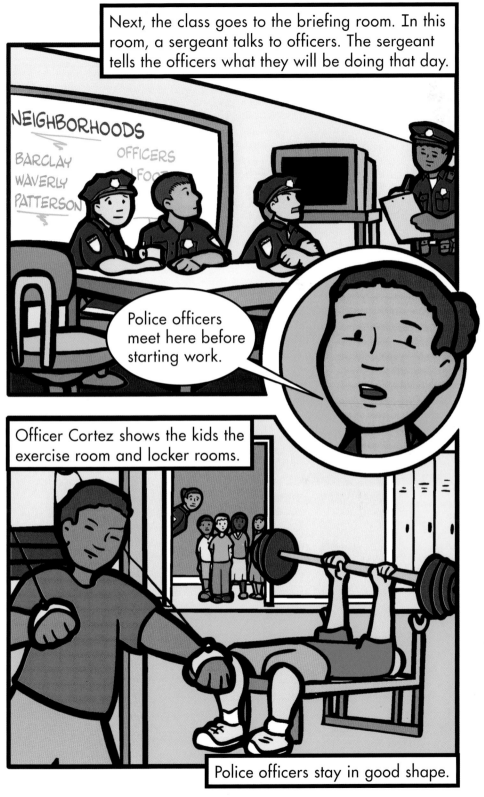

Next, the class goes to the briefing room. In this room, a sergeant talks to officers. The sergeant tells the officers what they will be doing that day.

NEIGHBORHOODS

BARCLAY
WAVERLY
PATTERSON

OFFICERS

Police officers meet here before starting work.

Officer Cortez shows the kids the exercise room and locker rooms.

Police officers stay in good shape.

11

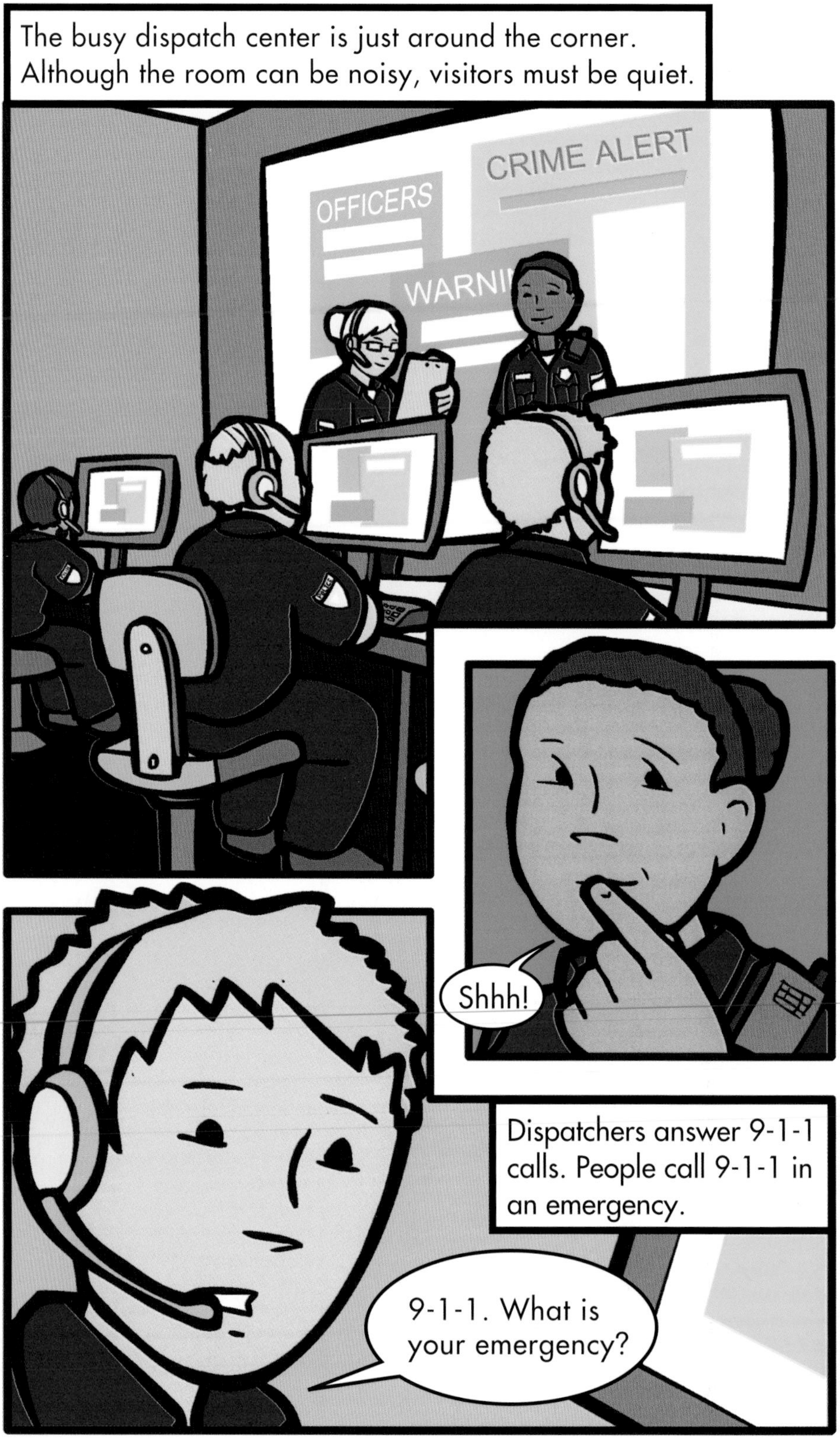
The busy dispatch center is just around the corner. Although the room can be noisy, visitors must be quiet.
CRIME ALERT
OFFICERS
WARNI
Shhh!
Dispatchers answer 9-1-1 calls. People call 9-1-1 in an emergency.
9-1-1. What is your emergency?

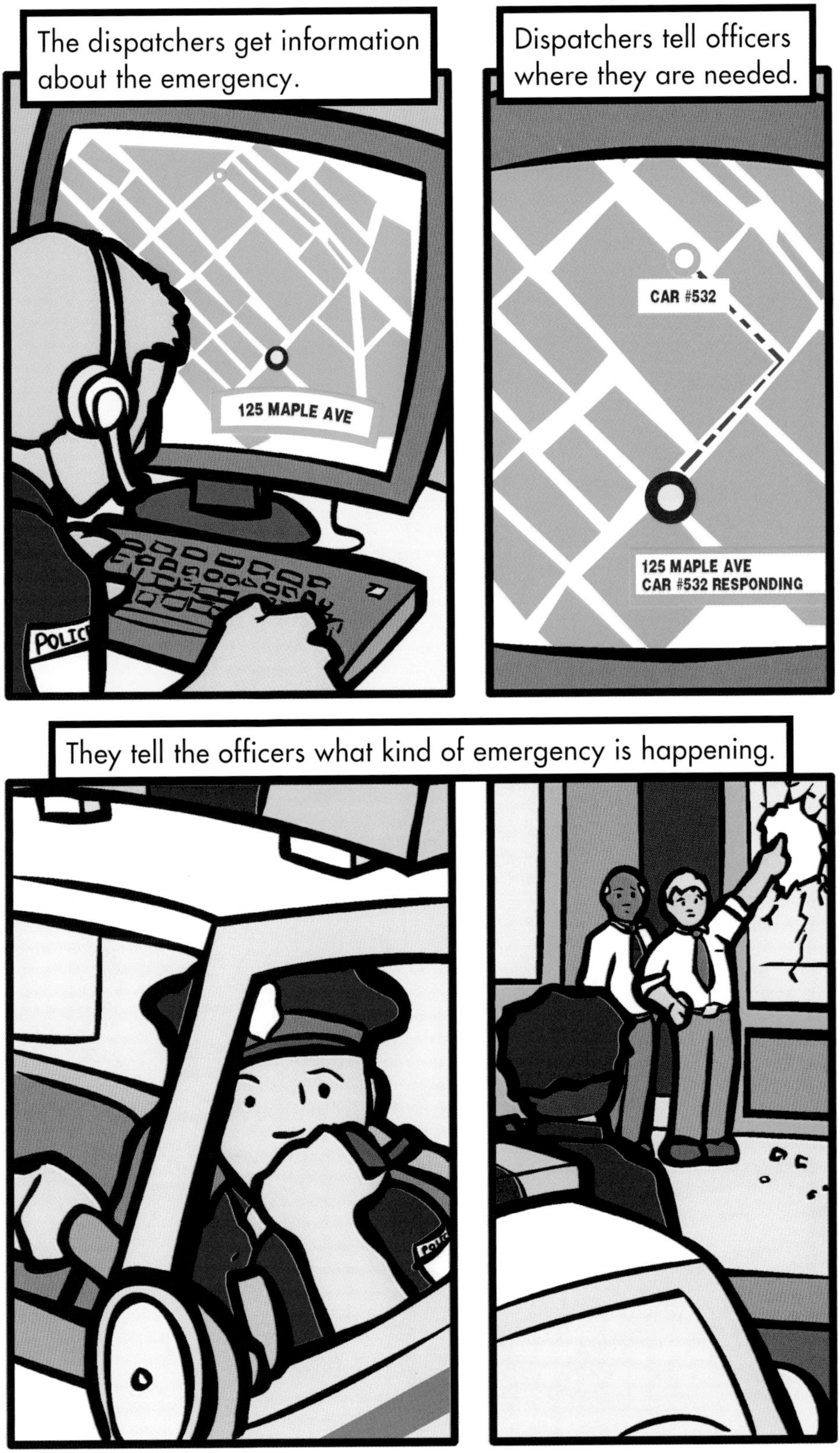
The dispatchers get information about the emergency.
125 MAPLE AVE
Dispatchers tell officers where they are needed.
CAR #532
125 MAPLE AVE
CAR #532 RESPONDING
They tell the officers what kind of emergency is happening.

IN THE SALLY PORT

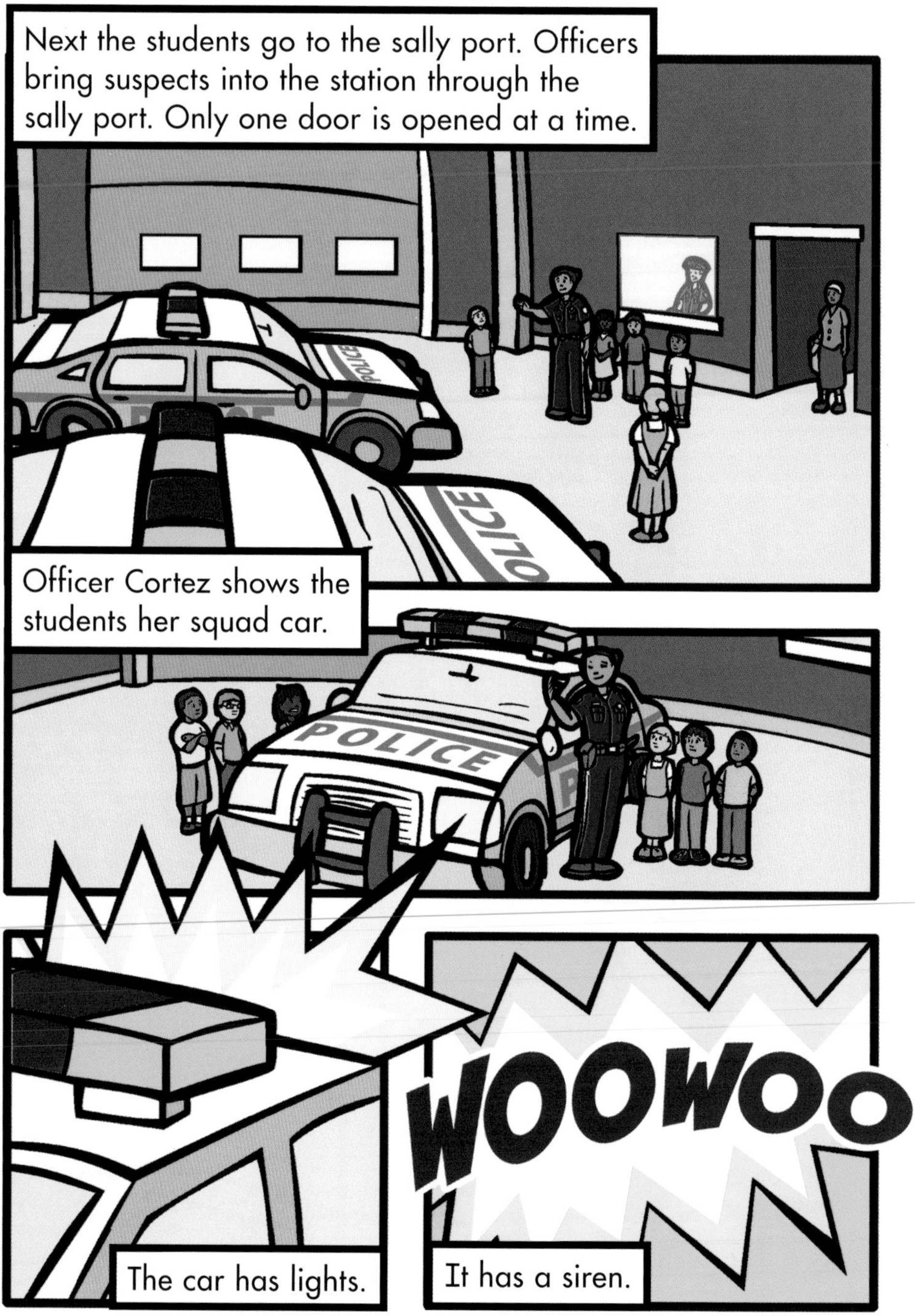
Next the students go to the sally port. Officers bring suspects into the station through the sally port. Only one door is opened at a time.
Officer Cortez shows the students her squad car.
POLICE
The car has lights.
WOOWOO
It has a siren.

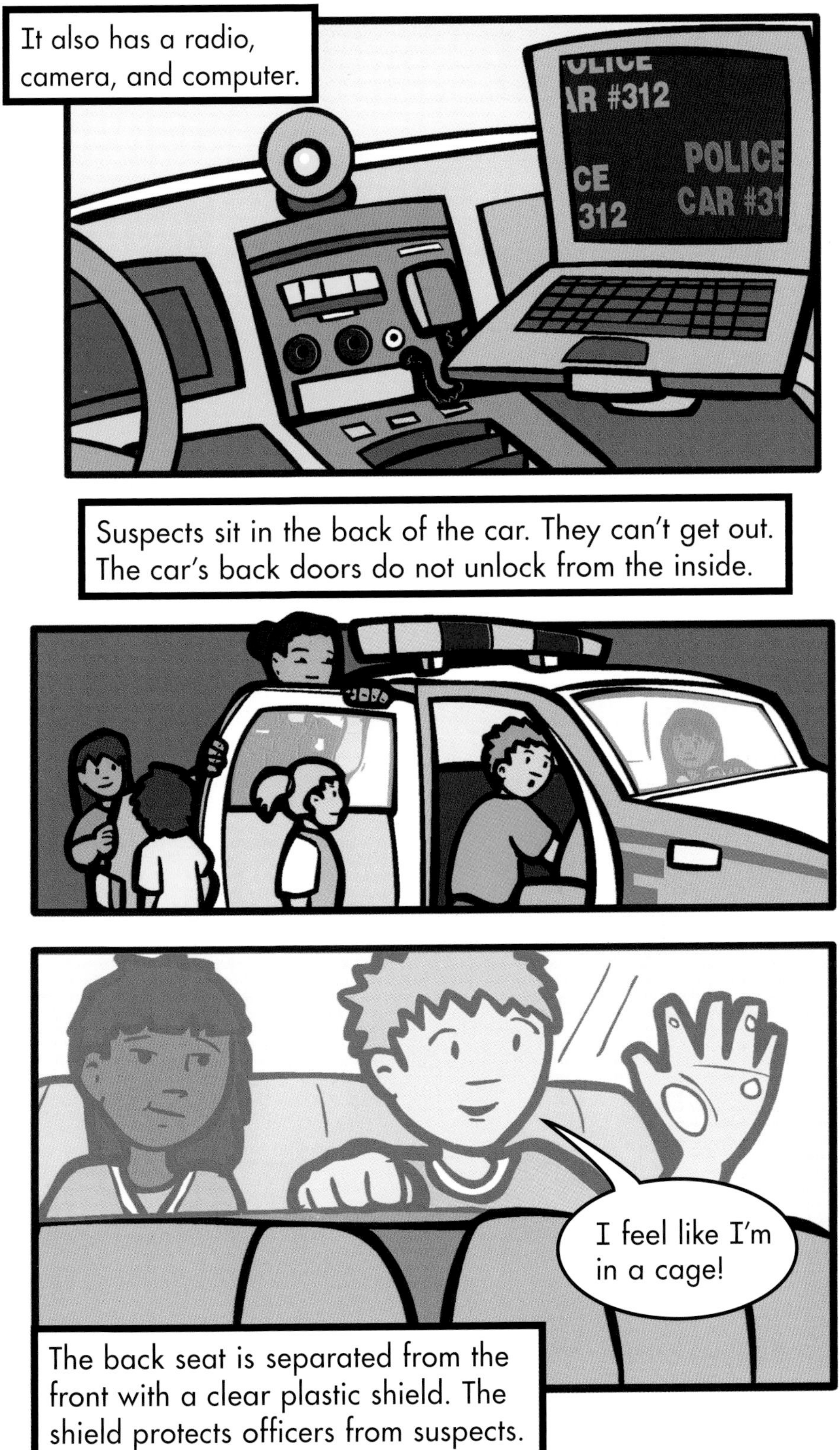
It also has a radio, camera, and computer.
Suspects sit in the back of the car. They can't get out. The car's back doors do not unlock from the inside.
I feel like I'm in a cage!
The back seat is separated from the front with a clear plastic shield. The shield protects officers from suspects.

Locked Up

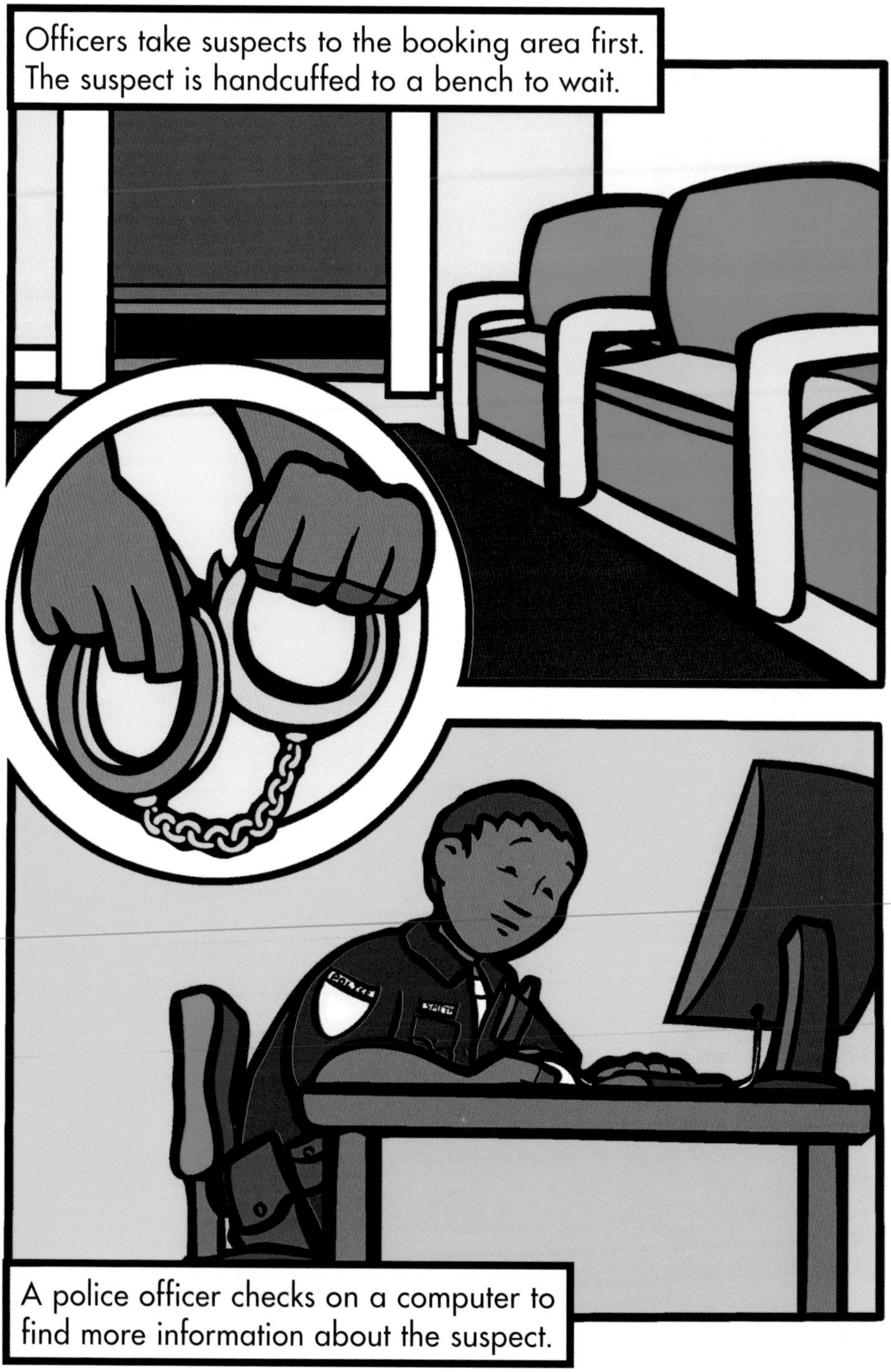
Officers take suspects to the booking area first. The suspect is handcuffed to a bench to wait.
A police officer checks on a computer to find more information about the suspect.

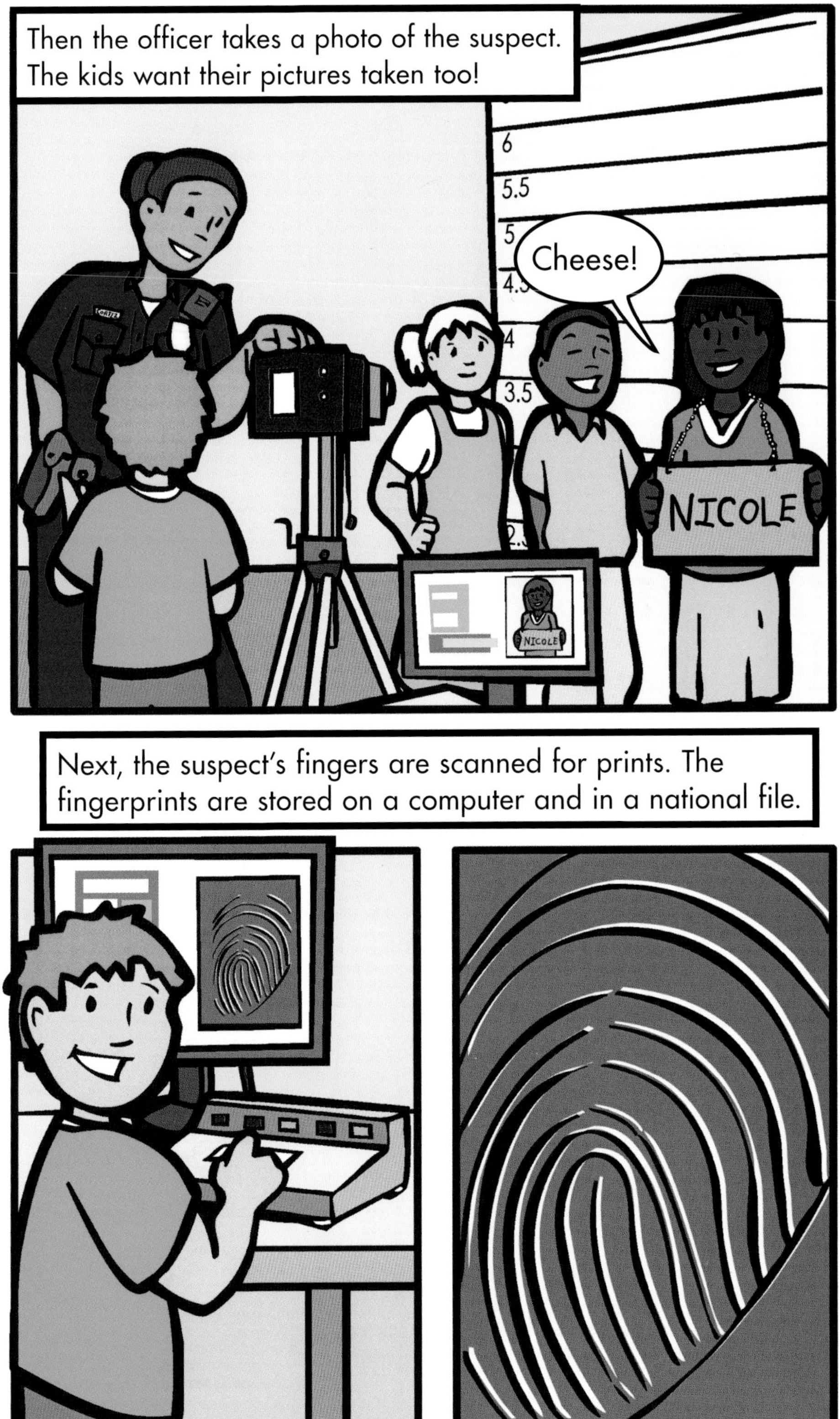
Then the officer takes a photo of the suspect. The kids want their pictures taken too!
Cheese!
NICOLE
Next, the suspect's fingers are scanned for prints. The fingerprints are stored on a computer and in a national file.

Sometimes officers take a suspect to a holding cell.

The cell is smaller than most bedrooms.

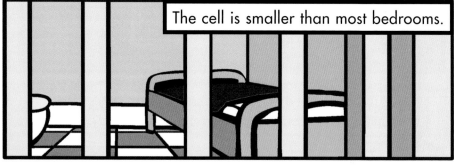

It has only a bed, sink, and toilet.

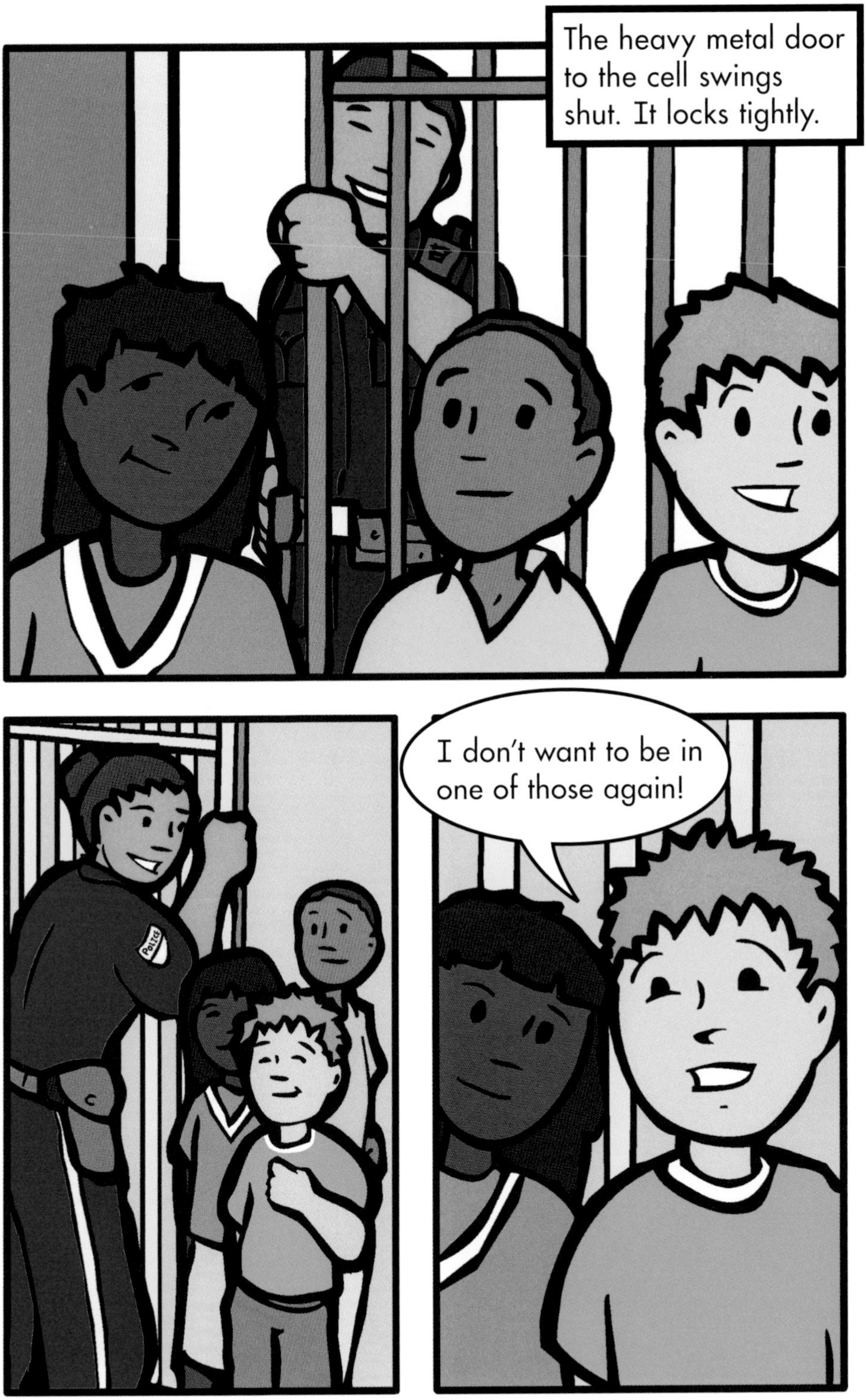
The heavy metal door to the cell swings shut. It locks tightly.
I don't want to be in one of those again!

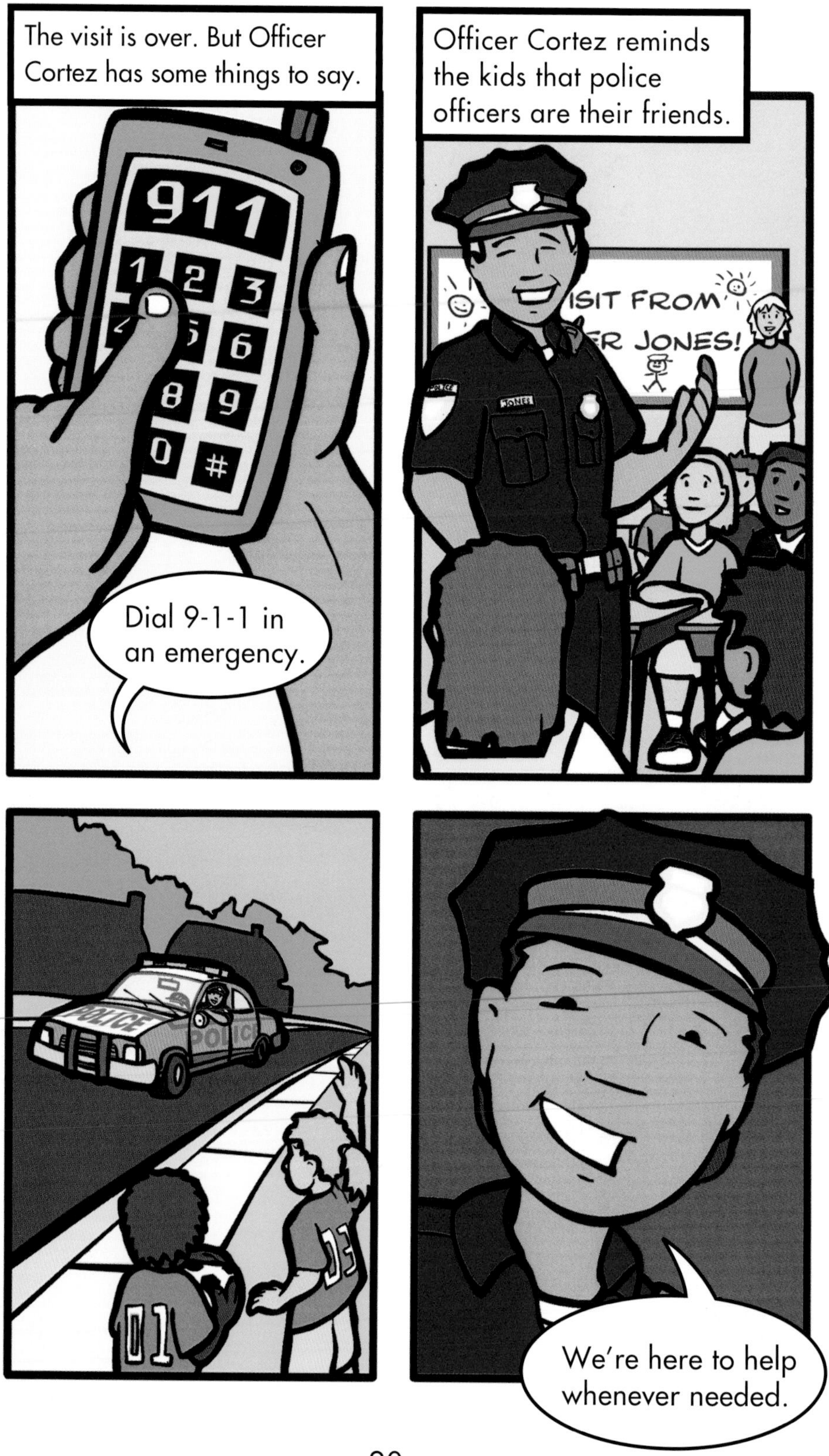
The visit is over. But Officer Cortez has some things to say.
Dial 9-1-1 in an emergency.
Officer Cortez reminds the kids that police officers are their friends.
We're here to help whenever needed.

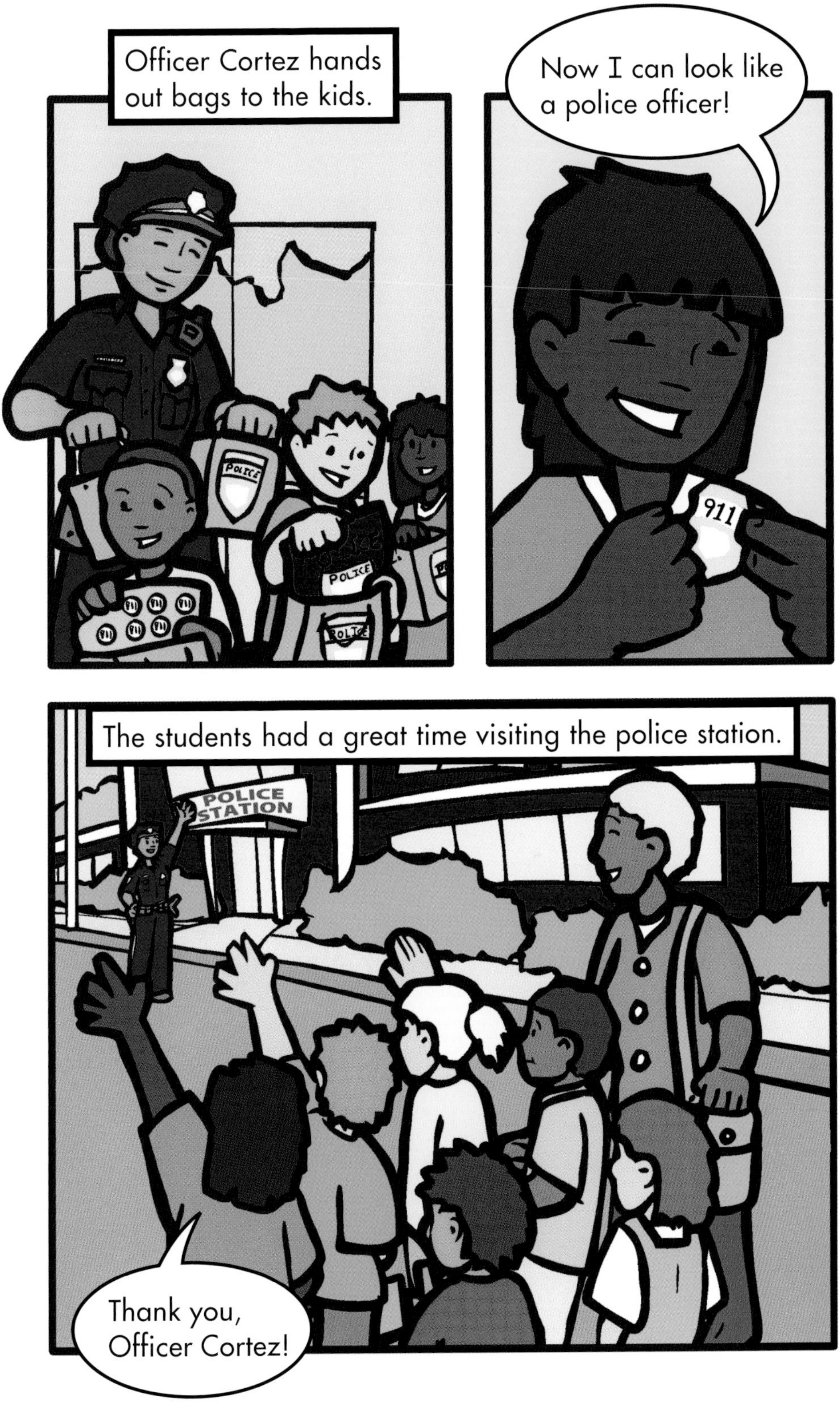
Officer Cortez hands out bags to the kids.
Now I can look like a police officer!
911
The students had a great time visiting the police station.
POLICE STATION
Thank you, Officer Cortez!

GLOSSARY

arrest—to stop and hold someone who may have broken a law

cell—a small locked room; some cells have bars

crime—something that is against the law

dispatcher—a person who answers 9-1-1 calls and assigns rescue workers

emergency—a sudden or dangerous event

fingerprint—a copy of the lines on the fingertips; used to identify someone

patrol—to protect and watch an area

scan—to move a beam of light across fingers to record the prints

sergeant—officer in charge of other patrol officers

suspect—someone who may be responsible for a crime

READ MORE

Ames, Michelle. *Police Officers in Our Community*. On the Job. New York: PowerKids Press, 2010.

Armentrout, David, and Patricia Armentrout. *The Police Station*. Our Community. Vero Beach, Fla.: Rourke Pub., 2009.

Leake, Diyan. *Police Officers*. People in the Community. Chicago: Heinnemann Library, 2008.

INTERNET SITES

FactHound offers a safe, fun way to find Internet sites related to this book. All of the sites on FactHound have been researched by our staff.

Here's all you do:

Visit *www.facthound.com*

Type in this code: 9781429653695

Super-cool stuff! Check out projects, games and lots more at **www.capstonekids.com**

INDEX

POLICE
POLICE

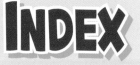

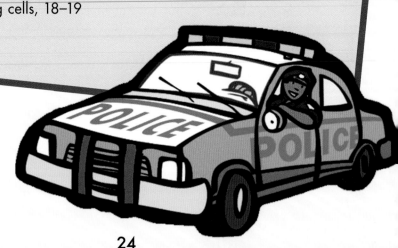

MY COMMUNITY

TITLES IN THIS SET:

- A DAY AT THE FIRE STATION
- GOING TO THE DENTIST
- TRANSPORTATION IN THE CITY
- A VISIT TO THE POLICE STATION
- A VISIT TO THE LIBRARY
- A VISIT TO THE VET
- WORKING ON THE FARM

FIRST GRAPHICS

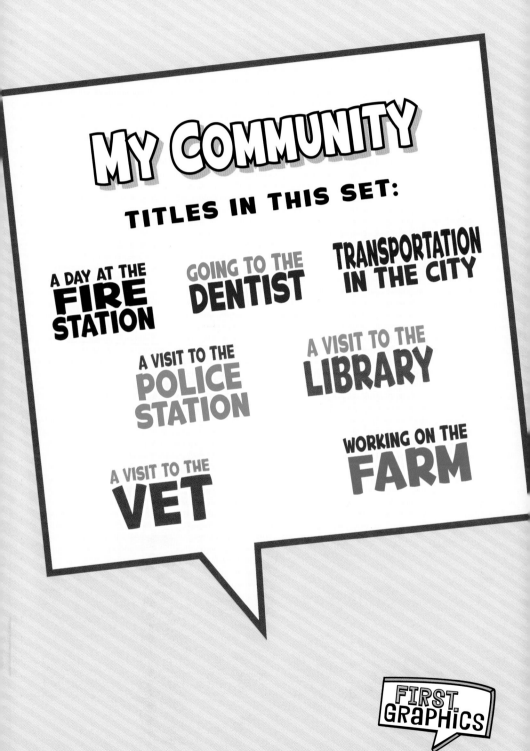